Map Workbook

for

WESTERN CIVILIZATION

VOLUME I

Cynthia Kosso
Northern Arizona University

Wadsworth
Thomson Learning™

Australia • Canada • Mexico • Singapore • Spain • United Kingdom • United States

ISBN 0-534-56844-0

For more information, contact
Wadsworth/Thomson Learning
10 Davis Drive
Belmont, CA 94002-3098
USA
http://www.wadsworth.com

International Headquarters
Thomson Learning
International Division
290 Harbor Drive, 2nd Floor
Stamford, CT 06902-7477
USA

UK/Europe/Middle East/South Africa
Thomson Learning
Berkshire House
168-173 High Holborn
London WC1V 7AA
United Kingdom

Asia
Thomson Learning
60 Albert Complex, #15-01
Singapore 189969

Canada
Nelson Thomson Learning
1120 Birchmount Road
Toronto, Ontario M1K 5G4
Canada

Contents

Notes

Introduction

Map reading is an important part of any person's basic knowledge about the world, whether for travel or keeping track of events around the world.[1] When someone gives you directions, or asks them of you, your brain automatically attempts to draw a rudimentary map. Your mind may even see roads as lines and rivers as bands or buildings as small squares. Maps are, of course, also useful for understanding history and geography. Maps tell us about the physical and cultural aspects of the world—and they can be deceiving. Colors and size can be used subtly to suggest "good guys" or "bad guys," or relative importance. In addition, maps have a long and interesting history.

A Brief History of Maps

Old maps and prints are fascinating because of their power to reflect the history of the world. When and where the very first maps were created is unknown. But clearly as soon as symbols were used, people felt the need to draw routes and illustrate their own territories. Among the earliest of known maps was one found in Turkey (Anatolia) at the site of Çatal Hüyük, dating to about 6300 BCE. This map, a wall painting, is a town plan, with a volcano looming in the background. Egyptians, Assyrians, and Babylonians also produced early maps and plans on papyrus and clay tablets. These were most likely land surveys for tax purposes. Controversy concerning the shape of the earth consumed philosophers from Anaximander to Strabo. Determining the shape of the earth, its size, habitable areas, climate zones and relative positions of regions preoccupied mapmakers over the centuries. Mathematicians, philosophers, and astronomers all sought answers to these problems. Plato, Herodotus, and Aristotle thought the world was round, an idea that eventually took hold in the Hellenic world. From our point of view, Strabo plays an important role in preserving the story of early map developments, though he misinterpreted the calculations made by Eratosthenes and Posidonius concerning the circumference of the earth. His work, *Geography*, is preserved in eight books and reveals sound geographic understanding. It also reveals an encyclopedic understanding of the countries and people of the Mediterranean region.

The Greek mathematician, Claudius Ptolemy, produced one of the most important early developments in map making. In ca. 150 CE, he collated all known information and

[1] I would like to thank the undergraduate students in the History of Western Civilization courses at Northern Arizona University. They provided indispensable help and advice in the development of my workbooks. I would also like to thank Kevin and Arthur Lawton for their editorial and content advice.

v

created his own *Geography* (another work in eight volumes). This work became the basis of mapping for about the next 1000 years and influenced the mapmakers who provided maps for explorers such as Columbus, Cabot, and Magellan. However, improvements in map making were slowed by the fall of the Roman Empire and the loss or dissipation of accumulated information. Increasing religious piety, and the belief in a flat world, forced the simplification of maps in Western Europe.

Following the Crusades, westerners were reintroduced to Ptolemy's work as well as the sophisticated mathematical knowledge of the Arabs which, fortunately, influenced later medieval mapmakers. Greek manuscripts from Constantinople were brought west, and once translated into Latin, began to intrigue scholars of historical geography. With the advent of printing, the production of numerous copies of maps became possible. The "age of discovery" brought more than discoveries of new lands—it brought the discovery of new geometric methods of survey and the invention of better instruments. Increasingly modern and recognizable maps were made. The Spanish and the Portuguese were particularly influential because of their fine early maritime charts (although, of course, at first these were kept very secret). In 1569, after advances in surveying technology had been made, the first Mercator maps were produced. As the quality of maps improved, they became art forms in their own right. Still, they contained numerous inaccuracies—California, for example, was drawn as an island.

During the 18th century the demand for maps grew stronger and both the middle classes and elites collected atlases, maps, new books, and similar luxuries. Many of these were huge folio maps, highly decorated. It was this elite market that began to demand more accuracy in map making, ultimately to the benefit of all. With the invention of steel engraving in the 19th century, mass production of maps became even easier. Maps were printed in large quantities and it was easier to keep them up to date. However, with an increase in accuracy, decoration became less common—slowly maps lost most of their decorative features as can be seen in modern maps, such as those in this workbook and in your atlases and texts. Aerial photography and satellite surveying have helped to furnish a wealth of detail hitherto missing from maps and these techniques have been used to enhance the accuracy and detail of all kinds of maps.

Defining Maps

In a way, maps are very simple. They are just a geographic region drawn on a flat surface. Typically, there are a number of commonly accepted standards and symbols used by all modern mapmakers. These symbols are defined in a key. In order to make the map (or to read one), a frame of reference is chosen. Within the frame of reference, a grid system, created by drawing the lines of latitude and longitude, helps to pinpoint locations accurately. Mapmakers chose the north and south poles as two definite, not arbitrary, points from which to begin dividing the world. Midway between these poles a line was drawn around the world (this is the **equator**). Next, lines were drawn parallel to the equator and moving toward each of the poles (the lines of **latitude**). To complete the grid, lines were drawn from pole to pole (the lines of **longitude**).

While the equator provides a natural line from which to measure, there is no such natural longitude line (although one was put in by convention and is called the prime meridian). A longitudinal starting point is obviously needed as a point of reference. The line through Greenwich, England is now most commonly used, but many nations have created maps with their own most important cities as reference points. The United States made maps with Washington, D.C., as the prime meridian. The Spanish drew their reference line through Madrid, the Greeks through Athens, the Dutch through Amsterdam, and so on.

Maps are designed with different scales—different proportions, or ratios, between the distance on the map and the actual distance on the world. The larger the fraction (or proportion), the smaller the territory covered. Inches per mile or centimeters per kilometer are the most common kind of **scale**. The scale is merely a fraction comparing the measures on the map (inches or centimeters) with the measures on the ground (miles or kilometers).

Finding the exact location of any place requires several steps. Reproducing the location accurately is complicated by the unavoidable distortion that arises from representing as a spatially flat surface, a region that lies on a round world. You may notice that the shapes of continents change slightly from map to map. This is because the distortion differs with the perspective of the map. Obviously, flat maps are not likely to be completely superseded by globes. Carrying a globe on a hike or road trip would be very inconvenient.

Map projections are the various ways in which one deals with the problem of distortion on a map of the earth's surface. The world is round. The map page is flat. All mapmakers, therefore, pick a perspective and a scale from which to display their particular purpose or orientation. For a map nearly devoid of distortion, one must have a spherical surface (this is known as a **globe**). Obviously, a flat map cannot perfectly represent a round surface. Typically a compromise is made whereby the directions, distances, and areas are drawn with the least inaccuracy possible to each. The **Mercator** maps are an example of how this works. The **Mercator** projection (as seen in the example above) is related to a cylindrical projection—that is, the mapmaker, or cartographer, works with the map as though it were a cylinder that circles the globe. Mercator maps, therefore, show the equator with great accuracy, while they distort the highest latitudes (this is known as the "Greenland problem").

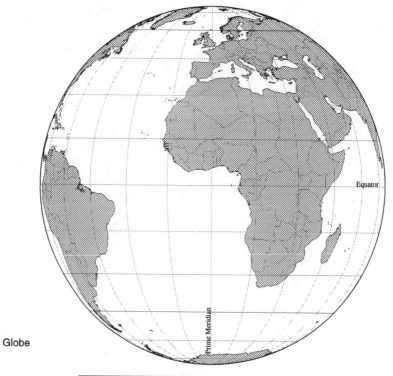

Globe

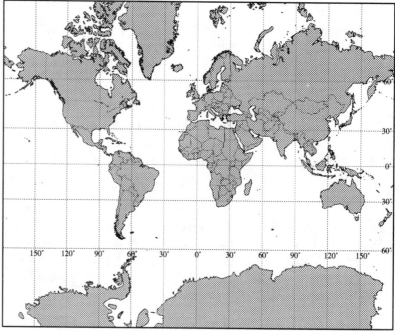

Mercator Projection

Map Perspectives

There are, as well, several kinds of maps. Hydrographic charts, used for navigation, show bodies of water and shores. Geologic maps show the physical structure of a region, while topographic maps show man-made and natural surface features in given regions. Political maps (as in the map of Europe below) traditionally show territorial boundaries and political divisions.

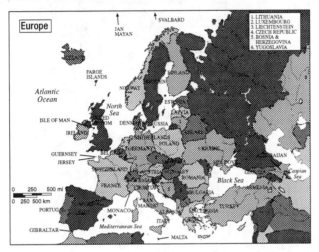

Political Europe

Climate maps (as seen in a climate map of Europe shown below) indicate the climates of various regions.

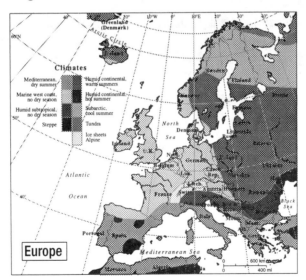

Europe Climate

And population maps (as seen in the example shown below of the population of Europe) describe the distribution of numbers of people among regions.

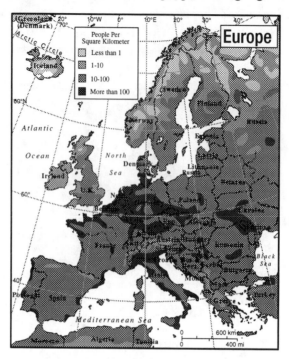

Europe Population

Every map, therefore, has a particular perspective. It has an author (the cartographer), a subject, and a theme. The subject in this exercise book is Western Civilization; themes vary from boundaries to distribution of religious groups. The subject and theme represent the author's interest, skills, political viewpoints, and historical context. Thus, maps represent only a version of reality. Maps are like snapshots of the world, a moment in time and space with a definite historical context. A nice example of perspective can be seen in one of the earliest maps known from the Babylonians. In this map, the Babylonians are situated precisely in the middle of the universe; all territories radiated from them—their own perception of the world.

A world map from the 16th century shows the continents as the Europeans knew them during this age of discovery. Compare a 16th century map to any later chart of the Americas and note how different in size and shape the continents are at different periods of time (clearly, the continents themselves did not change that much that quickly). The earlier world map reveals not only the author's knowledge of geography, but his interests—as indicated by the details he chose to include.

Still, in the search for accuracy and objectivity, one simply cannot add all details in all maps; the map would be rendered incomprehensibly complicated and useless. Nevertheless, maps are becoming increasingly accurate. Cartographers, especially since the late Middle Ages, have worked to perfect map making.

This map exercise book is designed to clarify the relationships among places and people through time—to help you to order events and historical locations. All sections incorporate several parts. Location sections ask you to find and correctly place a city, site, or other feature, or draw a boundary. Geography or environment sections require you to become familiar with the natural contours and context of a region. The human society and civilization sections ask you interpret human interactions with other civilizations and with the natural world. You will need to discuss and synthesize historical and geographical information in short essays. This workbook is intended to aid you in the study and understanding of how events, people, and natural processes relate to one another temporally.

Bibliography

Demko, George with Jerome Agel and Eugene Boe. 1992. *Why in the World, Adventures in Geography*. New York: Doubleday. This is a fun and easy to read introduction to mapping and geography. It does an excellent job of pointing out the importance of geography.

Greenhood, David. 1964. *Mapping*. Chicago: University of Chicago Press. This book provides a clear and concise introduction to maps and mapping.

Harley, J. B. and D. Woodward (eds.), *The History of Cartography*, University of Chicago Press (in press). Present the history of maps and mapping in several volumes.

Talbert, Richard J. A., "Mapping the Classical World: Major Atlases and Map Series 1872–1990," *Journal of Roman Archaeology* 5 (1992: 5–38. This article is especially interesting for students of ancient history.

Wood, Denis. 1992. *The Power of Maps*. New York: The Guilford Press. In this book Wood shows how maps are used and abused. It is an excellent introduction to the way maps have been used by groups and individuals to make an argument or present a point of view.

Useful Web Sites

http://www.pcclinics.com/maps/hist_sites.htm
http://www.maps.com

Part One: The Ancient World

The ancient world and western civilization developed in a world context and not as an isolated entity. Interactions among the various regions and people are evident from very early in human history. People traded with one another for food, tools and raw materials. In that process, they learned about one another, sometimes adopting practices, sometimes improving upon the technologies and customs that they found.

The First Civilizations: The Near East and Egypt

The earliest civilizations were found worldwide, in the valleys of the Fertile Crescent, India, China, and Egypt. Western civilization can be traced to the early societies of the Near East and Egypt. Mesopotamia, Greek for the "land between the rivers," was a rich land but difficult to farm. It took cooperation to build the irrigation systems needed to produce large quantities of agricultural goods. It was here that some of the earliest precursors to Western civilization were born. Writing, science, organized religion, and advanced technologies were a part of these civilizations. From the Near East and Egypt, we also get some of the earliest complex civilizations, with organized religion, public works projects, and writing. The Hebrews, a small tribe of people, provide us with a spiritual heritage out of proportion to their size. Small states gave way to empires and these gave way to new states and imperial systems. These states grew up around cities. Thus, the Near East and Egypt are home to some of the oldest urban centers on earth.

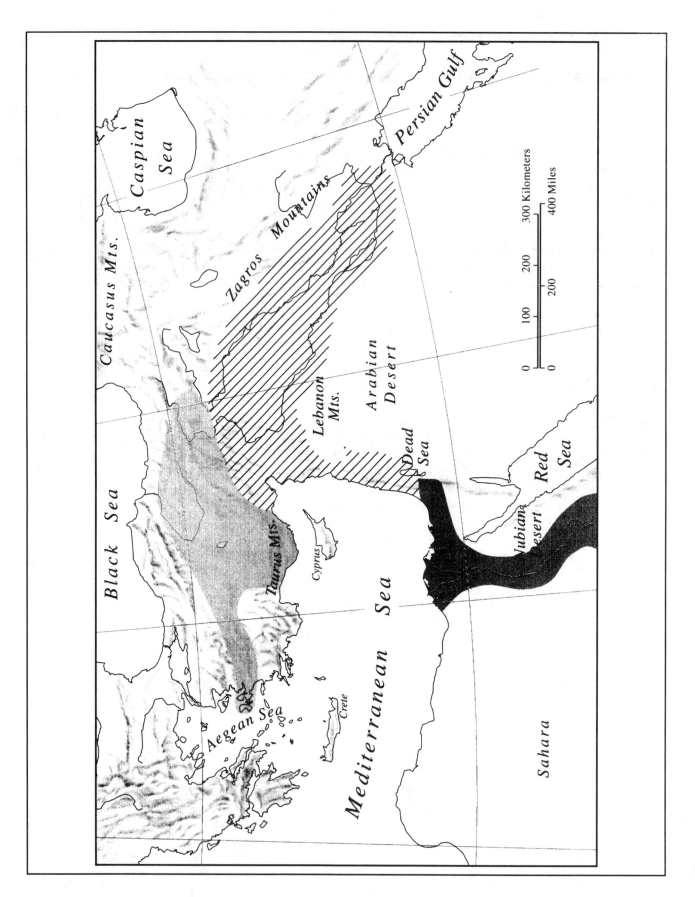

Caspian
Sea

Persian Gulf

Zagros Mountains

Caucasus Mts.

Black Sea

Lebanon Mts.

Arabian Desert

Dead Sea

300 Kilometers

400 Miles

200

200

100

Taurus Mts.

Cyprus

Red Sea

Nubian Desert

Mediterranean Sea

Aegean Sea

Crete

Sahara

Map 1

Locations

With different colored marking pens or pencils, place the number in the proper location and carefully shade in the regions and empires of the following peoples on Map 1. Also, place the numbers of the following Near Eastern and Egyptian cities on the map.

Cities

1. Amarna
2. Babylon
3. Çatal Hüyük
4. Giza
5. Jerusalem
6. Lagash
7. Memphis (Egypt)
8. Nineveh
9. Thebes (Egypt)
10. Uruk

11. Empires

12. Assyrian
13. Chaldean
14. Egyptian
15. Hittite
16. Persian

17. People

18. Mitanni
19. Philistines
20. Phoenicians

21. Regions

22. Akkad
23. Asia Minor
24. Assyria
25. Lower Egypt
26. Mesopotamia
27. Nile Delta
28. Parthia
29. Persia
30. Sinai
31. Sumer
32. Syria
33. Upper Egypt

Environment, Society, and Civilization: The Near East

1. How, when, and why did agriculture develop?

_____

_____

_____

_____

_____

_____

_____

_____

2. What are the major theories used to explain the existence and development of civilizations?

_____

_____

_____

_____

_____

3. What advantages and disadvantages do civilizations offer to us as human beings?

_____

_____

_____

_____

_____

4. From your reading, describe the physical environment of Çatal Hüyük and Babylon.

_____

_____

_____

_____

5. How do you think this environment affected the religious and political beliefs of the settlers at Çatal Hüyük and Babylon?

_____

_____

_____

_____

6. Briefly, discuss how the natural environment influenced the writing of the Mesopotamian creation myths and the Epic of Gilgamesh.

_____

_____

_____

_____

_____

7.	What political and religious factors made the Persians successful rulers of so many diverse peoples?

_____

_____

_____

_____

_____

_____

8.	What attracted Persians and Assyrians to the shores of the Mediterranean?

_____

_____

_____

_____

_____

9.	Briefly describe the different peoples living in Palestine in the first millennium BCE.

_____

_____

_____

_____

_____

10.	In a short paragraph, compare the religion of the Hebrews with that of its neighbors. How did the local environment influence the natures of these religions?

_____

_____

_____

_____

_____

_____

_____

Environment and Society: Egypt

11.   From your reading, describe the physical environment of the Nile Delta, and the cities of Thebes and Memphis

_____

_____

_____

_____

12.   What roles did the Nile and the Mediterranean play in the development of Egyptian society and economy?

_____

_____

_____

_____

13.   How did the Egyptian environment affect the political beliefs and behaviors of the Egyptians?

_____

_____

_____

_____

_____

14.   How is the Egyptian environment reflected in their beliefs? Please be as specific as possible.

_____

_____

_____

_____

15.   How did the environment of Egypt influence cultural developments? Please be as specific as possible.

_____

_____

_____

_____

Colonialism and Imperialism: Greece and Macedon

The world of the ancient Greeks was divided into many small city-states. Geography, especially the mountains and the sea, played an important role in their development. The islands of the Cyclades, which form a rough circle coming off the tip of Euboea and Attica, were inhabited very early. They were politically important for resources, strategy, and religion. Melos was the only local source of obsidian for weapons and surgical instruments. Delos was the home of Apollo and was sacred. On Crete an early Greek civilization flourished for more than a thousand years. Not infrequently, the states of the mainland used and depended upon the political and economic support of these island people. Empires in the region began with the conquests of the Athenians after the formation of the Delian League—which, though misused as a tool of expansion, was originally created as a defensive alliance of Greek states in opposition to the Persians. Alexander the Great elaborated the imperial system begun by the Athenians and changed the political map of the "civilized" world. His ambitions led him to conquer his neighbors on the Balkan Peninsula and then head to the east. He incorporated dozens of cultures and thousands of miles into his Macedonian Empire. The creation of this empire was hard won, but not long lasting. Upon Alexander's untimely death, his conquests were divided among his faithful generals.

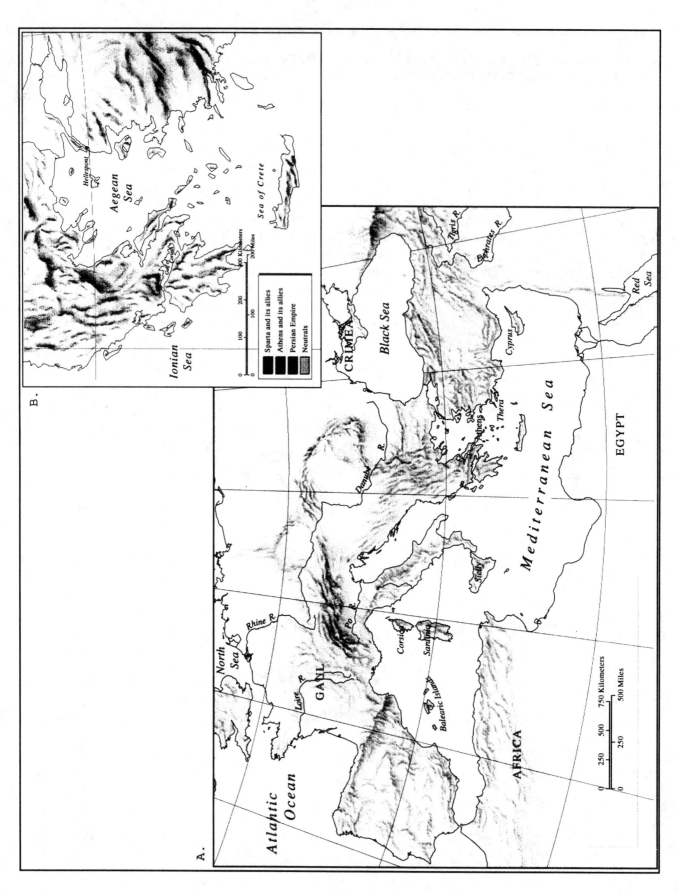

B.

Aegean Sea

Hellespont

Sea of Crete

Ionian Sea

Gulf of Corinth

100
100
200
200 Miles
200 Kilometers

Sparta and its allies
Athens and its allies
Persian Empire
Neutrals

A.

Atlantic Ocean

North Sea

Rhine R.

Loire R.

GAUL

Po

Corsica

Sardinia

Balearic Islands

AFRICA

250
250
500
500
750 Kilometers
500 Miles

Danube R.

CRIMEA

Black Sea

Tigris R.

Euphrates R.

Cyprus

Red Sea

Athens

Thera

Mediterranean Sea

Sicily

EGYPT

MAP 2

Locations: Greece and Macedon

Label the most appropriate insert to the left on Map 2. With different colored marking pens or pencils, shade in and place the number in the appropriate location for the following regions or islands, geographical features, and cities.

Regions

1. Asia Minor
2. Boeotia
3. Corcyra
4. Crete
5. Delos
6. Euboea
7. Ionia
8. Laconia
9. Lesbos
10. Macedonia
11. Melos
12. Naxos
13. Peloponnesos
14. Samos
15. Thera
16. Thessaly
17. Thrace

Cities

18. Argos
19. Athens
20. Corinth
21. Cyrene
22. Ephesus
23. Knossos
24. Miletus
25. Mycenae
26. Olympia
27. Persepolis
28. Sparta
29. Susa
30. Thebes
31. Troy
32. Tyre

Geographical Features and Regions

33. Aegean
34. Balkan Peninsula
35. Iberian Peninsula
36. Italy
37. Mt. Olympus
38. Nile River
39. Propontis
40. Sea of Crete

Environment

1. What role did geography play in the evolution of Greek history?

_____

_____

_____

_____

_____

_____

2.   How does the geography of Greece compare to that of Egypt and the Near East?

_____

_____

_____

_____

_____

_____

_____

_____

3.   What advantages and what disadvantages did the Greeks have because of their geographical location?

_____

_____

_____

_____

_____

_____

_____

_____

Human Society and Civilizations

4.   Describe the areas associated with the Minoan and Mycenaean cultures and give their approximate dates.

_____

_____

_____

_____

_____

5.   The Greeks were rarely a quietly settled people. Using the discussion on colonization in your text, describe the areas settled by the Greeks and the Phoenicians and give the dates of settlement.

_____

_____

_____

_____

_____
_____
_____
_____
_____
_____

6.   When and where did the colonization movement begin?

_____
_____
_____
_____
_____

7.   Why did the Greeks choose to colonize where they did?

_____
_____
_____
_____
_____

8.   What human and environmental factors contributed to the successful campaigns of Alexander the Great?

_____
_____
_____
_____
_____
_____
_____

9.   What were the long-term effects of Alexander's conquests on the areas that he captured?

_____
_____
_____
_____
_____
_____
_____

Life in Greece

10. Imagine that you are a foreign slave in Classical Athens. Write a brief essay on the circumstances that led to your enslavement, where you came from and carefully describe the routes you traveled to arrive in Athens.

_____
_____
_____
_____
_____
_____
_____
_____
_____
_____
_____
_____
_____
_____
_____
_____
_____
_____
_____
_____
_____
_____
_____
_____
_____
_____
_____
_____
_____
_____

Imperialism Perfected: Rome and Its Empire

The Romans forged one of the world's longest lasting imperial systems—in ancient or modern history. They created a legacy that we all share. It all began on the Italian peninsula in a little village on the banks of the Tiber River. After the conquest of the Italian peninsula, the Romans began to interact more aggressively with their more distant neighbors. Beginning in the Western Mediterranean, the Romans gained territory rapidly and forcefully. Among the most famous of all the wars fought by the Romans were the Punic wars with the Carthaginians. One of the greatest Carthaginian generals was Hannibal—among the few who attacked the Romans on their own territory in these early days of Roman growth.

Despite internal social and political upheavals, the Romans managed to forge a strong and enduring political system. After an imperial system of government was in place, the Romans continued to expand their lands. New territories were needed to bring in more income. As regions were added to the Empire, the need for an efficient and regulated administration grew. Wisely, and whenever possible, the Romans co-opted existing systems of management. The Roman approach to control of subject people tended to smooth the transition to membership in the Empire and reduced the chances of rebellion and dissatisfaction.

ℰ

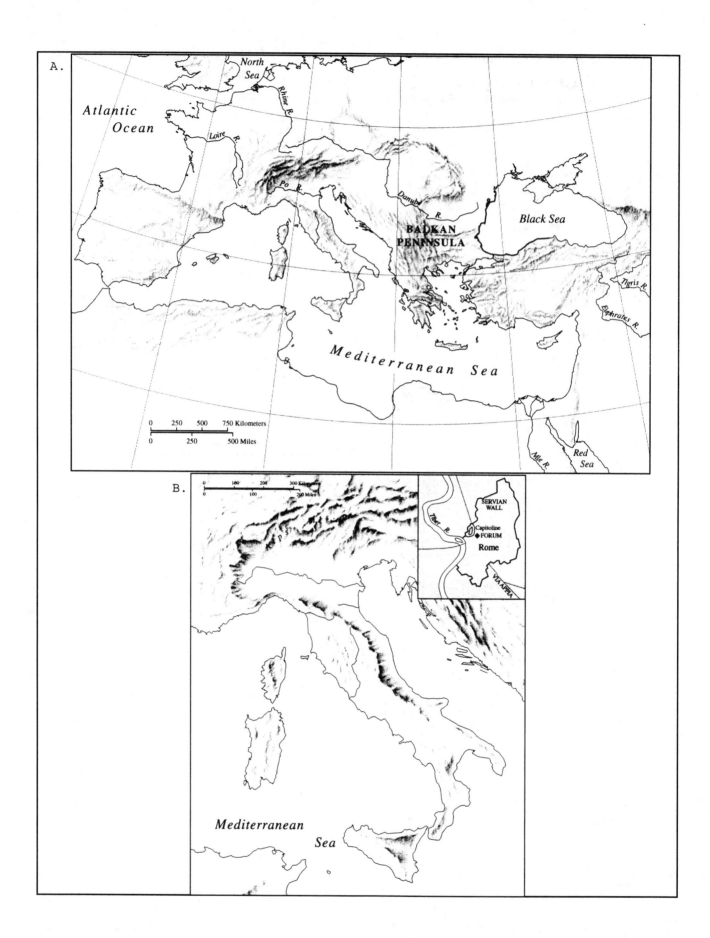

A.

North Sea

Atlantic Ocean

Rhine R.

Loire R.

Po R.

Danube R.

BALKAN PENINSULA

Black Sea

Tigris R.

Euphrates R.

Mediterranean Sea

Nile R.

Red Sea

| 0 | 250 | 500 | 750 Kilometers |
| 0 | | 250 | 500 Miles |

B.

| 0 | 100 | 200 | 300 Kilom. |
| 0 | | 100 | 200 Miles |

SERVIAN WALL

Tiber R.

Capitoline
FORUM

Rome

VIA APPIA

*Mediterranean
Sea*

MAP 3

Locations

With different colored marking pens or pencils, locate the proper number on Map 3 for the following cities, and approximately shade in and number the following regions and geographical features.

Cities and Battle Sites

1. Brindisi
2. Cannae
3. Cumae
4. Cynoscephalae
5. Messina
6. Naples
7. Rome
8. Saguntum
9. Syracuse
10. Tarentum
11. Trasimene
12. Veii
13. Zama

Regions, Provinces and Frontiers

14. Africa
15. Arabia
16. Asia
17. Britain
18. Carthage
19. Cisalpine Gaul
20. Dacia
21. Etruria
22. Greece
23. Illyria
24. Judaea
25. Latium
26. Macedonia
27. Magna Graecia
28. Numidia
29. Sardinia
30. Scotland
31. Sicily
32. Spain

Geographical Features

33. Adriatic Sea
34. Apennine Mts.
35. Arno River
36. Po River
37. Rhône River
38. Rubicon River
39. Taurus Mts.
40. Tiber River

Environment

1. What areas in Italy provided the best agricultural land?

_____

_____

_____

_____

_____

_____

_____

2.	What other resources did the peninsula provide the Italians?

_____

_____

_____

_____

_____

3.	Compare the geography of Italy to the Greek peninsula.

_____

_____

_____

_____

_____

4.	What natural advantages did Italy possess over Greece and how did this affect their respective histories?

_____

_____

_____

_____

_____

_____

_____

5.	What were the main natural and man-made resources from Spain, Greece, Egypt, Sicily and Northern Africa?

_____

_____

_____

_____

_____

_____

_____

_____

_____

_____

Human Society and Civilizations

6.   Why were the Romans interested in the western Mediterranean? The Eastern?

_____
_____
_____
_____
_____

7.   Why were cities so important to the Romans? Describe the various functions that they served.

_____
_____
_____
_____
_____

8.   What were the major differences between the cities of the eastern and western empire?

_____
_____
_____
_____
_____

9.   How were the provinces and frontiers of the Roman Empire governed and protected?

_____
_____
_____
_____

10.   What were the long-term effects of Roman rule on the provinces of the western empire?

_____
_____
_____
_____
_____

The Ancient World: Test Your Knowledge

A.   For each of the following regions list the major natural resources and available manmade products.

1.   Asia Minor

_____

_____

_____

_____

_____

2.   England

_____

_____

_____

_____

_____

3.   Gaul/France

_____

_____

_____

_____

_____

4.   Italy

_____

_____

_____

_____

5.   Spain

_____

_____

_____

_____

_____

B.   For each of the following empires, briefly describe the territorial boundaries at their greatest extent:

6.   Assyrian Empire

_____
_____
_____
_____
_____

7.   Neo-Babylonian Empire

_____
_____
_____
_____
_____

8.   Empire of Alexander the Great

_____
_____
_____
_____

9.   Roman Empire in the Late Republic

_____
_____
_____
_____
_____

10.   Roman Empire of the Emperor Trajan

_____
_____
_____
_____
_____

C.   Match the geographical feature on the left with the region on the right with which it is most accurately associated:

Adriatic Sea	Asia Minor
Aegean Sea	Egypt
Alps	Egypt/Arabian Peninsula
Taurus Mts.	Gaul
Dead Sea	Greece
Nile	Israel
Pyrennes Mts.	Italy
Red Sea	Italy/Illyria
Tiber	Mesopotamia
Tigris	Spain

Part Two: Late Antiquity and the Middle Ages

The Roman political system dissolved in the western provinces and was replaced by smaller kingdoms, empires, and principates. In the east, however, Roman government remained stable and despite invasions and migrations was able to forge a long lasting Late Roman or "Byzantine" state. The Middle Ages, therefore, developed very differently in the east and west. The western regions were transformed by the influences of German, Celtic, Slavic, and other traditions. The East, while not untouched by new ideas, maintained ancient Greek and Roman traditions, even in the face of strong Arab and Islamic pressure.

Competing Empires: Byzantines and Carolingians

The Frankish (Merovingian) kingdom controlled the old Roman province of Gaul for several centuries. This was a united Christian kingdom. By the seventh century, however, the kingdom was divided and beginning to weaken. As a result, Charles Martel, the mayor of the palace of Austrasia, gained power and, most importantly, defeated the Muslims at Poitiers. But it was his son, Pepin, who, with the help of the Catholic Church, would depose the Merovingians and create a new Frankish kingdom—that of the Carolingians. The Pepin's son, Charlemagne (or Charles the Great) was the most renowned and powerful of the Carolingian leaders.

In the eastern half of the old Roman Empire the government remained stable and powerful. This Eastern Roman Empire has become known as the Byzantine Empire, although the people continued to consider themselves "Roman." The emperors of the east treated the Germans in the west as regents of Roman power. In the sixth century, however, a real attempt was made to reunite the old empire into a territorial and institutional whole. The Emperor Justinian was the mastermind behind this plan, and he was partially and temporarily successful. Friction, not unnaturally, resulted from conflicting ideas about the nature and ownership of power in the west.

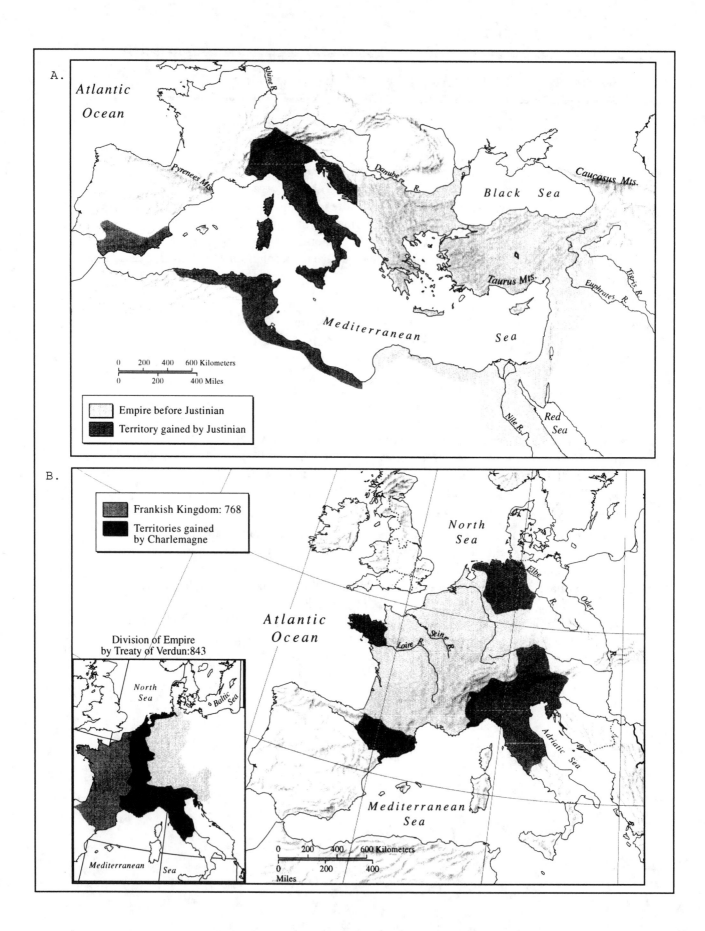

A.

Atlantic Ocean

Rhine R.

Pyrenees Mts.

Danube R.

Black Sea

Caucasus Mts.

Taurus Mts.

Euphrates R.

Tigris R.

Mediterranean Sea

Nile R.

Red Sea

	Empire before Justinian
	Territory gained by Justinian

0   200   400   600 Kilometers

0   200   400 Miles

B.

	Frankish Kingdom: 768
	Territories gained by Charlemagne

North Sea

Elbe R.

Oder R.

Atlantic Ocean

Loire R.

Seine R.

Adriatic Sea

Division of Empire by Treaty of Verdun: 843

North Sea

Baltic Sea

Mediterranean Sea

Mediterranean Sea

0   200   400   600 Kilometers

0   200   400 Miles

MAP 4

Locations

On the appropriate inset on Map 4, using different colors for each group, shade in the boundaries and number the territories of the new western kingdoms listed below. Also number and place on the map cities and geographical features listed below.

Kingdoms and Regions

1. Alemanni
2. Arabia
3. Austrasia
4. Bulgars
5. Burgundy
6. Celts
7. Franks
8. Kingdom of Sicily
9. Lombards
10. Mercia
11. Neustria
12. Ostrogoths
13. Picts
14. Vandals
15. Visigoths

Cities

16. Aachen
17. Belgrade
18. Bordeaux
19. Constantinople
20. Cracow
21. Danzig
22. Leipzig
23. Nuremberg
24. Paris
25. Verdun

Byzantine Neighbors

26. Alemanni
27. Arabia
28. Bulgars
29. Burgundians
30. Ostrogoths
31. Persian Empire
32. Syria

Geographical Features

33. Baltic Sea
34. Danube River
35. Rhine River

Environment

1.   What were the material and environmental advantages of the territories held by Justinian?

_____

_____

_____

_____

_____

_____

_____

2.   Describe the major trade routes in the Byzantine Empire.

_____
_____
_____
_____
_____
_____
_____

3.   What, and from where, were the major goods being imported? Exported?

_____
_____
_____
_____
_____

4.   What affect did the location of Constantinople have on trade in the Byzantine Empire?

_____
_____
_____
_____
_____

5.   Describe the environmental difficulties encountered by the agricultural populations in the era of the Carolingians.

_____
_____
_____
_____
_____

6.   Describe the major trade routes of the Carolingians.

_____
_____
_____
_____
_____
_____

Human Society and Civilizations

7.   What were the main socio-political characteristics of the Byzantine Empire in the eighth century? And how do they relate to the geographical context of the Byzantine world?

_____

_____

_____

_____

_____

8.   In the west, what were the long-term political and economic results of the Treaty of Verdun?

_____

_____

_____

_____

9.   Describe the linguistic and cultural differences that were emerging in the divided territories of the Carolingian Empire.

_____

_____

_____

_____

_____

_____

10.   What nations would emerge from the Carolingian territories?

_____

_____

_____

_____

11.   List at least five of the major regions of the Holy Roman Empire. Try to explain these divisions of the Holy Roman Empire. Did they help or hinder stability in the empire? Explain.

_____

_____

_____

_____

_____

_____

Life in the Byzantine and Carolingian Worlds

12.   Imagine that you are a merchant from Constantinople and that you are traveling to the Carolingian court. Write an essay describing what sorts of goods might you be trading and your impressions of daily life in Early Medieval Europe. Note especially the things that differ most dramatically from your own experiences in the east.

_____

_____

_____

_____

_____

_____

_____

_____

_____

_____

_____

_____

_____

_____

_____

_____

_____

_____

_____

_____

_____

_____

_____

_____

_____

_____

_____

_____

_____

New People: Goths, Germans, and Slavs

As we have seen, the Roman political system was weakened in the western provinces; in Eastern Europe, it eventually was replaced by numerous small Germanic and Slavic kingdoms. A few of these kingdoms like the Carolingians would prove to be fairly long lived. The Christian Church also benefited from the withdrawal of Roman power from the west. Some form of Christianity was accepted by most of the German people who gained the old Roman territories. Around the territories on each side of the Oder River, there was considerable intermixing of German with Slavs (which, incidentally, resulted in instability in Polish borders which characterized Poland well into the twentieth century).

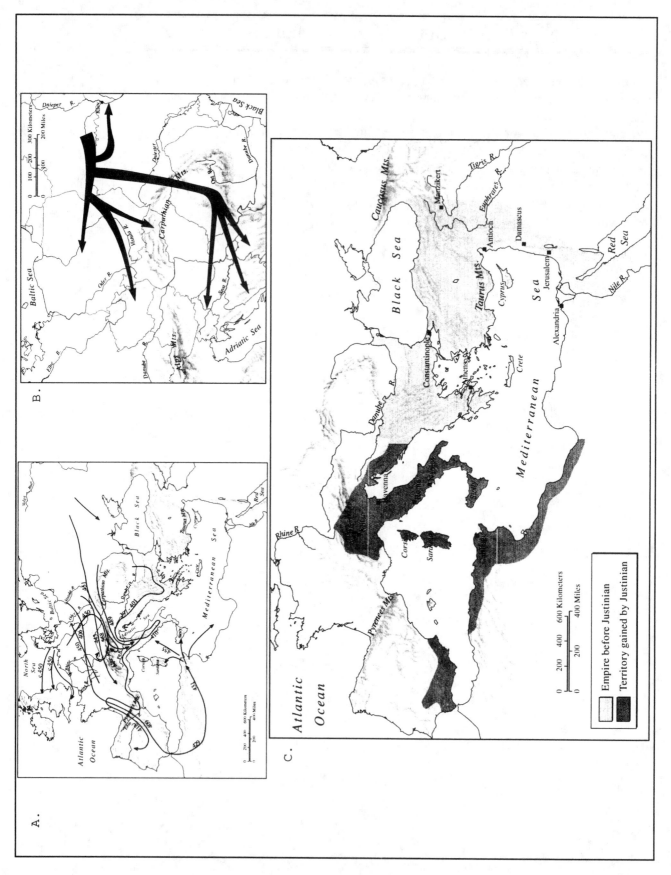

A.

B.

C.

Empire before Justinian

Territory gained by Justinian

MAP 05

Locations

Migrating and invading people took over the territories of the former Roman Empire in the west. On the appropriate inset on Map 5, using different colors for each group, lightly shade in the territories of and number the following successor groups. On the other maps, label the migrations of the Slavs, and the "Barbarian" migration and invasion routes:

Kingdoms

1. Alemanni
2. Celts
3. Franks
4. Lombards
5. Merovingians
6. Picts
7. Saxons
8. Scots
9. Vandals

Germanic Peoples

11. Franks
12. Huns
13. Ostrogoths
14. Vandals
15. Visigoths

Environment

1.   How did the environment and geography of Europe contribute to the migrations and invasions of the Germanic, Gothic, and Slavic peoples?

_____
_____
_____
_____
_____
_____
_____
_____
_____
_____
_____
_____
_____
_____
_____

2.   What cultural characteristics of the Germans can you identify as having an environmental explanation?

_____

_____

_____

_____

_____

_____

3.   What cultural characteristics of the Slavs can you identify as having an environmental explanation?

_____

_____

_____

_____

_____

_____

Human Society And Civilizations

4.   What were the main causes of friction between the ancient Italian peoples and their German rulers?

_____

_____

_____

_____

_____

_____

_____

5.   How did German law and society differ from that of the ancient Romans? In what ways was the natural world a contributor to these differences?

_____

_____

_____

_____

_____

_____

_____

6.   What long term impact did the German and Slavic people have on the development of political systems and territorial boundaries in the west?

_____
_____
_____
_____
_____
_____

7.   What long term cultural impact did the German and Slavic people have on the west?

_____
_____
_____
_____
_____
_____

8.   Briefly summarize the family structure of the ancient Franks.

_____
_____
_____
_____
_____
_____

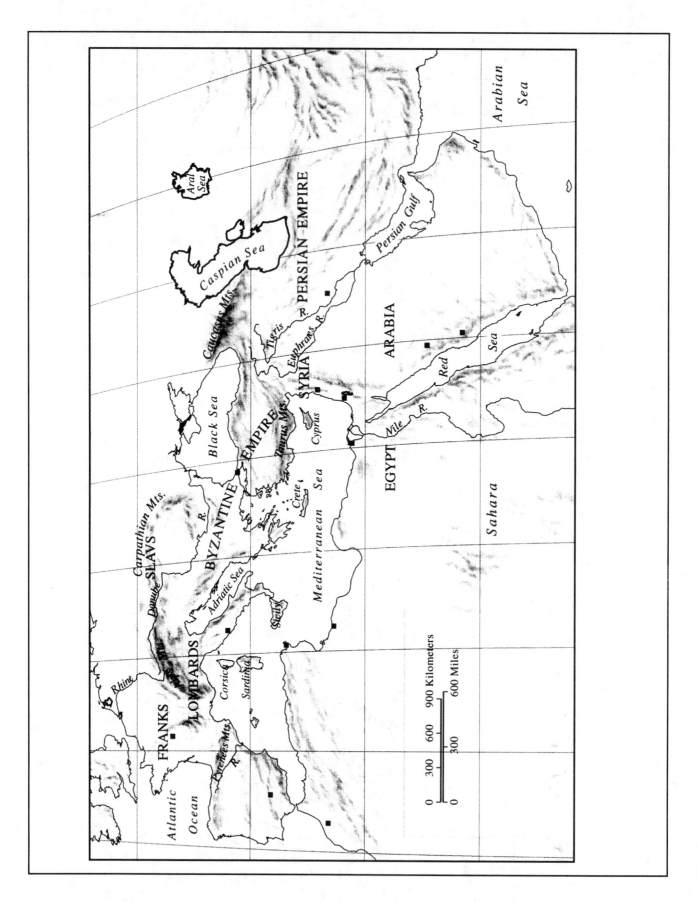

MAP 6

New Ideas: Christianity and Islam

The Roman political system in the western provinces was eventually replaced by numerous small Germanic kingdoms, and the Christian Church benefited from the withdrawal of Roman power. Some form of Christianity was accepted by most of the German people who gained the old Roman territories. This exercise locates the German successor states and identifies important Christian centers.

In the seventh century, Arab tribes began to accept a new religion, Islam, and to expand their influence in both the eastern and western Mediterranean world. The acceptance of Islam by the Arabs was rapid and complete. The reasons for such a rapid and successful religious revolution are still not clear. Upon unifying politically as well as religiously, the Arabs began to expand their territory.

Locations

On Map 6, shade in and label the territories gained by Islamic peoples by about 632. In another color, shade in and label the territories held by 661. Finally, in a third color, shade in and label the territories held through Islamic expansion by 750 CE. Also, place the number or name of the following cities on your map:

1. Alexandria
2. Antioch
3. Baghdad
4. Cordoba
5. Jerusalem

6. Mecca
7. Medina
8. Poitiers
9. Tripoli
10. Tunis

Environment

1. What impact did geography have on the spread of Christianity in Europe? Be specific.

_____
_____
_____
_____
_____

2.   What impact did geography have on the spread of Islam in the Middle East, Africa, and Europe? Be specific.

_____

_____

_____

_____

_____

_____

_____

_____

_____

Human Society And Civilizations

3.   Name at least five major centers of Christian diffusion in the western territories. Describe the locations of these centers and explain their importance.

_____

_____

_____

_____

_____

_____

_____

_____

_____

_____

4.   Name at least five major centers of Christian diffusion in the eastern territories. Describe the locations of these centers and explain their importance.

_____

_____

_____

_____

_____

_____

_____

_____

_____

5.   Briefly, describe the routes and processes of the Christianization of Britain.

_____

_____

_____

_____

_____

_____

6.   In the sixth and seventh centuries, the Latin Christian church gained considerable power and prestige. Name at least two reasons why this was so.

_____

_____

_____

_____

_____

_____

7.   What factors enabled the territorial expansion of Islam on such a large scale?

_____

_____

_____

_____

_____

8.   What factors or events stopped the territorial expansion of Islam into Christian Europe?

_____

_____

_____

_____

_____

9.   What impact did the Islamic conquests have on Christian Europe?

_____

_____

_____

_____

_____

35

Life in the Islamic World

10.   Using your texts and other sources, write an essay describing how the advent of Islam changed the roles of women in Arabic society. Be sure to clarify the status of women before the birth of Muhammed (ca. 570 CE). At the end of your essay, please properly cite any sources that you used.

_____

_____

_____

_____

_____

_____

_____

_____

_____

_____

_____

_____

_____

_____

_____

_____

_____

_____

_____

_____

_____

_____

_____

_____

_____

_____

_____

_____

Late Antiquity and the Middle Ages: Test Your Knowledge

Next to each of the following regions and cities, write in its associated religion and the approximate date of conversion to that religion. When the region underwent more that one conversion, e.g., from pagan to Christian to Muslim, you will need to list all major conversions and their dates.

1. Aachen _____

2. Alexandria _____

3. Antioch _____

4. Canterbury _____

5. Cologne _____

6. Cordoba _____

7. Ephesus _____

8. Fez _____

9. Marseilles _____

10. Mecca _____

11. Medina _____

12. Milan _____

13. Nicaea _____

14. Paris _____

15. Tours _____

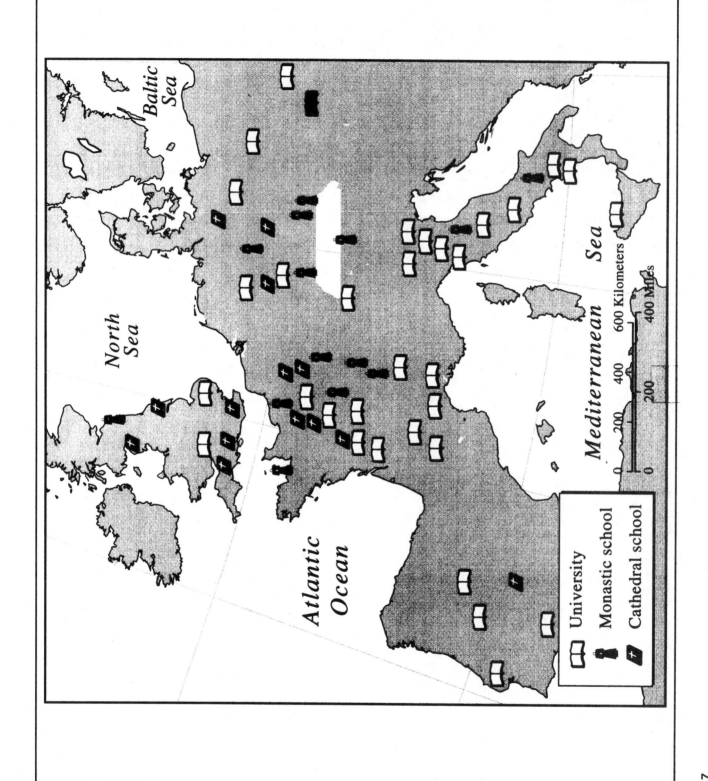

Baltic Sea

North Sea

Atlantic Ocean

Mediterranean Sea

University
Monastic school
Cathedral school

0   200   400   600 Kilometers
0   200   400 Miles

MAP 7

Part Three: Late Middle Ages to the Reformation

The 12th through the 16th centuries saw a myriad of rapid, and profoundly influential, developments. Technological transformations, the creation of universities, population fluctuations and the infusion of dramatically new ideas led to the foundations of modern religious divisions and systems of government. There were a variety of reasons for these changes, including but not limited to, new ways of thinking imported from the east though peaceful trade and the violence of the Crusades, dislocations caused by the Black Death, (which was a disaster of enormous magnitude), and conflicts within and surrounding the Catholic church.

The Spread of New Ideas: Education

Intellectual life in the later Middle Ages reflected a period of exceptional vitality and change. The clergy, hitherto the main educators in the European world, began to lose some of their dominance and influences in education began to be felt from the work of secular officials, warriors, courtiers, philosophers and aristocrats. The university, in its modern form, developed during this era in order to train both an educated clergy and educated secular citizenry.

Locations

On Map 7, place the appropriate city center next to its university, monastic school, or cathedral school icon.

1. Bologna	6. Naples	11. Reims
2. Cambridge	7. Notre Dame	12. Rome
3. Chartres	8. Oxford	13. Seville
4. Durham	9. Paris	14. Toledo
5. Mainz	10. Prague	15. Vienna

Society and Civilization

1. Briefly, list five of the earliest major Universities with the date of their foundation.

_____
_____
_____
_____
_____
_____

2. What were the origins of these schools? Why did schools arise in the locations that they did?

_____
_____
_____
_____
_____
_____

3. What physical and educational characteristics did these early universities share?

_____
_____
_____
_____
_____

4. Can you explain why there were fewer universities in Spain than in France?

_____
_____
_____
_____
_____

5. What effect did the humanist movement have on education and the locations of schools?

_____
_____
_____
_____
_____

Life In A Medieval University

6.   Imagine that you are a student in Bologna. Write a letter to your father describing your location and experiences.

_____

_____

_____

_____

_____

_____

_____

_____

_____

_____

_____

_____

_____

_____

_____

_____

_____

_____

_____

_____

_____

_____

_____

_____

_____

_____

_____

_____

_____

_____

_____

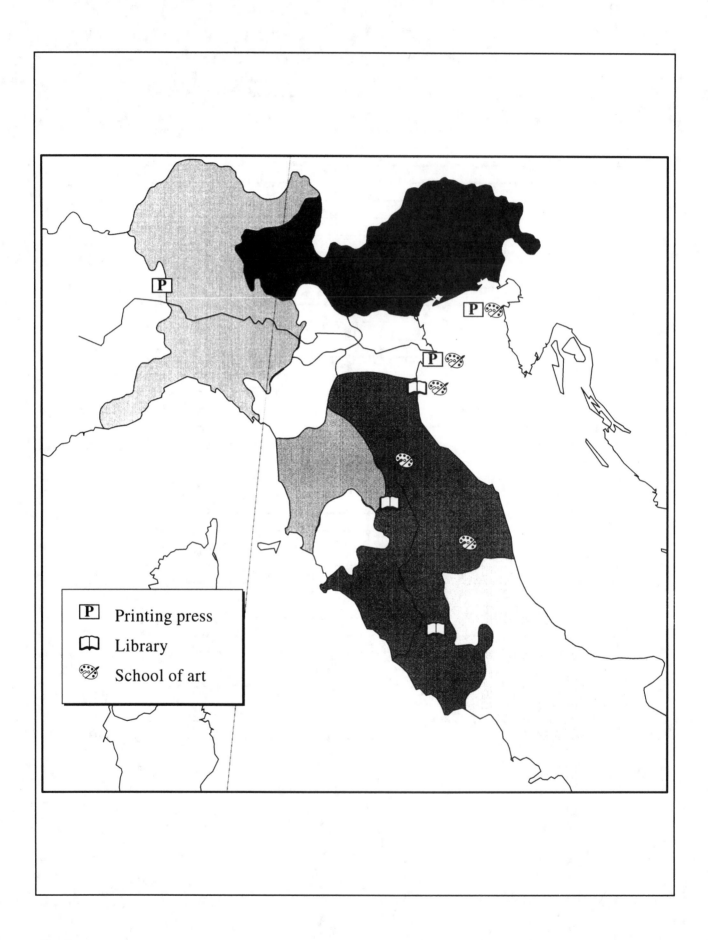

P   Printing press

📖   Library

🎨   School of art

MAP 8

Culture and Politics: Italy and the Renaissance

State systems varied by region and era. For example, though in the fourteenth century Italy had a well-established system of city-state governments, often in conflict with one another, by the fifteenth century there were only a few, very powerful states left. They vied with one another for a variety of reasons, often calling on the Papacy or the Holy Roman Empire of the Germans to support their claims. Frequent warfare was the result, and unification of nations such as Italy was a long way away. Europe had entered a period of turmoil and rebirth exemplified by political rivalries as well as intellectual and artistic achievements of the Renaissance and Reformation.

Locations

On Map 8, next to the symbols for presses, libraries, and schools of art, write the name of the associated city. In the proper area, also write in the following regions:

Duchy of Ferarra	Papal States
Duchy of Milan	Republic of Florence
Duchy of Modena	Republic of Lucca
Duchy of Savoy	Republic of Siena
Kingdom of Naples	Republic of Venice

Culture And Society

1.   How did the five major 15th-century powers in Italy come to dominance?

_____
_____
_____
_____
_____
_____
_____
_____
_____

2.   What role did geography play in the development of these regional powers?

_____

_____

_____

_____

_____

_____

_____

3.   Compare and contrast the Renaissance of Italy and the Northern Renaissance. In what ways were these "rebirths" most similar and in what ways were they most different?

_____

_____

_____

_____

_____

_____

_____

4.   How did geography and location affect regional developments? Be specific.

_____

_____

_____

_____

_____

_____

5.   Using Renaissance recipes and menus as guides, discuss how trade in Renaissance Italy affected the daily lives of the elite.

_____

_____

_____

_____

_____

_____

Politics and Religion: The Reformation

In contrast to Italy, Spain was home to several independent Christian nations that had managed, militarily, to take the peninsula from those practicing Islam and Judaism. The Spanish enforced strict orthodoxy. Unlike the leaders and states of Italy, Isabella of Castile and Ferdinand of Aragon made major progress toward early unification of the Iberian Peninsula. Their combined power and wealth, plus the support of the Catholic Church would make them a real threat to countries near and far. Yet, at the same time the Christian church in the sixteenth century was suffering from the consequences of abuses by Catholics (in particular the papacy) and was reaching a crisis point. Many reform movements grew out of the frustration of the times; some made surprisingly influential by the dissemination of these new ideas through the written word, now easily spread because of the printing press. The Reformation in Germany led by Martin Luther was to be one of the most influential. It was not long before the populations of Europe had chosen sides: Protestant (e.g., Lutheran, Calvinist, Anglican) or Catholic.

1.   Compare and contrast the Reformation in England and Germany. How did local conditions affect the different approaches to reformation?

_____
_____
_____
_____
_____
_____
_____
_____
_____

2.   What impact did the Reformation generally have on the economy of Europe? Give several examples.

_____
_____
_____
_____
_____
_____
_____
_____
_____

3.   What impact did the Reformation have on the political life and territorial boundaries of Europe? And, on the other hand, what impact did existing territorial divisions have on the progress of the Reformation?

_____
_____
_____
_____
_____
_____
_____
_____
_____
_____

4.   What impact did the Reformation have on the society of Europe? Give several examples.

_____
_____
_____
_____
_____
_____
_____
_____
_____

5.   Next to the following cities, list the appropriate religious affiliation (Anglican, Calvinist, Calvinist influenced, Roman Catholic, Lutheran, Lutheran influenced).

A.   Amsterdam _____

B.   Cologne _____

C.   Dijon _____

D.   Edinburgh _____

E.   Geneva _____

F.   London _____

G.   Madrid _____

H. Oxford   _____

I. Paris   _____

J. Rome   _____

K. Seville   _____

L. Trent   _____

M. Vienna   _____

N. Wittenberg   _____

O. Worms   _____

Life and Death in the Middle Ages

The Black Death killed from 25 to 50% of the population of Europe. In some cases, entire villages were wiped out. Some cities saw their populations reduced by more than half. The disaster had cultural, economic and religious results.

6.   Briefly describe the nature of the Black Death and outline its progress through Europe.

_____

_____

_____

_____

_____

_____

_____

_____

_____

7.   How did the environment of Europe influence the progress of the Black Death?

_____

_____

_____

_____

_____

_____

_____

8.   Discuss European responses to the Black Death. What were some of the psychological and religious responses experienced by the inhabitants of Europe? Give specific examples.

_____

_____

_____

_____

_____

_____

_____

_____

_____

9.   What economic ramifications did the Black Death have? Be detailed.

_____

_____

_____

_____

_____

_____

_____

_____

_____

10.   In what ways did the Black Death have long term political effects?

_____

_____

_____

_____

_____

_____

_____

_____

_____

Late Middle Ages to the Reformation: Test Your Knowledge

Next to the name listed below, list the individual's date, major achievements or characteristics, and main location of activity:

1. Botticelli, Sandro

_____

_____

_____

_____

2. Charles V (Holy Roman Emperor)

_____

_____

_____

_____

_____

3. da Vinci, Leonardo

_____

_____

_____

_____

_____

4. della Mirandola, Pico

_____

_____

_____

_____

5. di Donatello, Donato

_____

_____

_____

_____

_____

6.   Dufay, Guillaume

_____
_____
_____
_____
_____
_____

7.   Erasmus, Desiderius

_____
_____
_____
_____
_____
_____

8.   Gutenberg, Johannes

_____
_____
_____
_____
_____
_____

9.   Henry VIII

_____
_____
_____
_____
_____
_____

10.   Hus, John

_____
_____
_____
_____
_____
_____

11.   Isabella of Castile

_____

_____

_____

_____

_____

_____

12.   King Louis XI of France

_____

_____

_____

_____

_____

_____

13.   Loyola, Ignatius

_____

_____

_____

_____

_____

_____

14.   Luther, Martin

_____

_____

_____

_____

_____

_____

15.   Michelangelo

_____

_____

_____

_____

_____

_____

16. More, Thomas

_____

_____

_____

_____

_____

17. Pope Paul III

_____

_____

_____

_____

_____

18. Prince Ivan III

_____

_____

_____

_____

_____

19. Raphael

_____

_____

_____

_____

_____

20. Zwingli, Ulrich

_____

_____

_____

_____

_____

Part Four: Early Modern Europe

After the Reformation swept Europe a system of secular states began to appear. Absolutist monarchs tried to stabilize the boundaries and societies of the European states. After the end of the Thirty Years' War, however, Germany was still made up of more than three hundred independent states, each vying for power and territory. The Holy Roman Empire was an entity in name only. Out of the hundreds of German states, two became most powerful: Brandenburg and Austria. Both of these states would grow and strengthen because of particularly dominating families, the Hohenzollerns and the Hapsburgs respectively. Political change led to local disruptions and rebellions.

Expansion, Crises, and Enlightenment

In 1492, a new era in world history was launched. European adventurers took their ships in search of wealth, fame and new worlds to conquer and convert. These men provoked a transformation of Africa, Asia, the America's and Europe itself. A ferment of ideas and scientific advances furthered European efforts to explore and dominate the entire world. The English, French, Spanish, Portuguese and Dutch all fanned out to conquer and colonize the old and New World. Discoveries and conquests of rich and unusual lands and people kept Europeans interested in the foreign travel and control. Settlements and ports were founded along the coasts of Africa. Across the Atlantic, the Spanish especially, established rich and vast empires, conquering and killing huge numbers of Amerindians in the process, and then replacing these indigenous people with imported slave laborers from Africa.

Back at home, divine-right kings dominated European states in the 16th century. Cultural and political differences remained, however, and these led to very different forms of government as the centuries passed. England, for example, eventually created a constitutional monarchy, while France was ruled, absolutely, by the "Sun King" from his magnificent palace at Versailles.

Yet the ideals of the Enlightenment were professed by all alike: constitutional as well as absolute monarchs. Austria was ruled by an "enlightened" monarch who tried hard to reform government and, in particular, tried to limit the power of the Catholic

Church. Peter the Great, and then, Catherine the Great of Russia, likewise tried to turn toward the west's ideas of enlightened rule and at the same time use the west for trade and technology.

℘

Politics and Place

1.   List and give the dates for the main voyages of discovery in the 15th and 16th centuries.

A. _____

B. _____

C. _____

D. _____

E. _____

F. _____

G. _____

H. _____

I. _____

2.   What territories in the New World were under Spanish control by the 16th century?

_____

_____

_____

_____

_____

3.   What territories were under Portuguese control by the 16th century?

_____

_____

_____

_____

_____

_____

4.   How were the New World territories administrated?

_____

_____

_____

_____

_____

_____

5.   What problems arose in the new territories because of the vast distances to the homelands?

_____

_____

_____

_____

_____

_____

6.   Write an essay discussing the short and long-term impact of European settlement on the people and environment of the New World. What impact did the discovery of these territories have on the countries and people of Europe?

_____

_____

_____

_____

_____

_____

_____

_____

_____

_____

_____

_____

_____

_____

_____

_____

_____

_____

_____

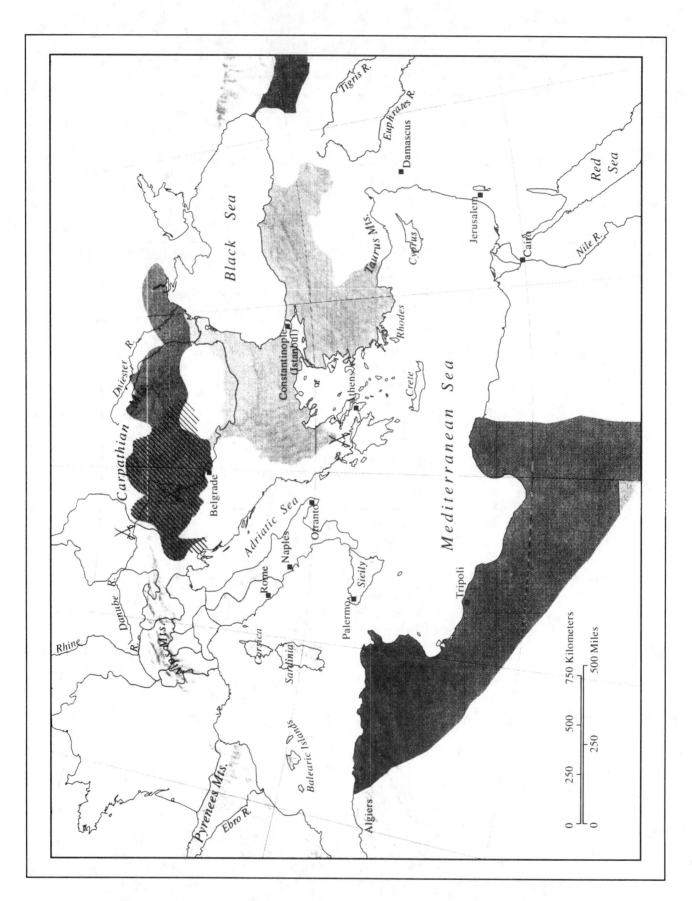

Tigris R.

Euphrates R.

Damascus

Red Sea

Black Sea

Taurus Mts.

Jerusalem

Cairo

Nile R.

Dniester R.

Cyprus

Constantinople (Istanbul)

Rhodes

Carpathian

Athens

Crete

Mediterranean Sea

Belgrade

Adriatic Sea

Otranto

Rhine

Danube R.

R.

Mts.

Rome

Naples

Palermo

Sicily

Tripoli

Corsica

Sardinia

Balearic Islands

Algiers

Pyrenees Mts.

Ebro R.

250   500   750 Kilometers

250   500 Miles

0

0

MAP 9

East and West: Ottomans in Europe

The Turkish people, led by the Ottomans, conquered the Byzantine Empire once and for all in 1453 with the capture of Constantinople. This was a tremendous victory and afterwards the Turks were on the move. They added vast tracts of lands to their wealthy empire. The Ottomans were very effective at getting the Europeans to accept them as an equal power. They had an intricate and effective government, with a strong and well-organized military. This exercise traces the growth of Ottoman strength and influence in Europe and the Mediterranean regions.

Locations

On Map 9 . . .

—Place the following names and dates alongside the appropriate battle symbols:

1. Vienna, 1683
2. Lepanto, 1571
3. Mohacs, 1526

—In the proper shaded regions, place the extent of Ottoman territorial gains in:

4. 1451
5. 1481
6. 1521
7. 1566
8. Also, label the territories lost to the Ottomans in 1699.

—Finally, label your map with the following regions:

9. Anatolia
10. Aragon
11. Moldavia
12. Papal States
13. Switzerland
14. Transylvania
15. Wallachia

Society and Civilizations

1.   After 1566, the northern boundaries of the Ottoman Empire were relatively fixed. What occurred to stop further movement into Northern Europe?

_____

_____

_____

_____

_____

_____

2.   What were the strengths and weaknesses of the Ottomans?

_____

_____

_____

_____

_____

_____

3.   How were these strengths and weakness linked to their territories?

_____

_____

_____

_____

_____

_____

4.   What were the long-term results of their conquests?

_____

_____

_____

_____

_____

_____

_____

_____

_____

_____

_____

_____

Technology and Change: The Industrial Revolution

In the 18th century the economic and social structure of Europe was transformed. New forms and sources of energy and power, combined with an abandonment of traditional forms of labor, were the basis of the "Industrial Revolution." The Industrial Revolution changed society, families, culture and the economy in a myriad of ways.

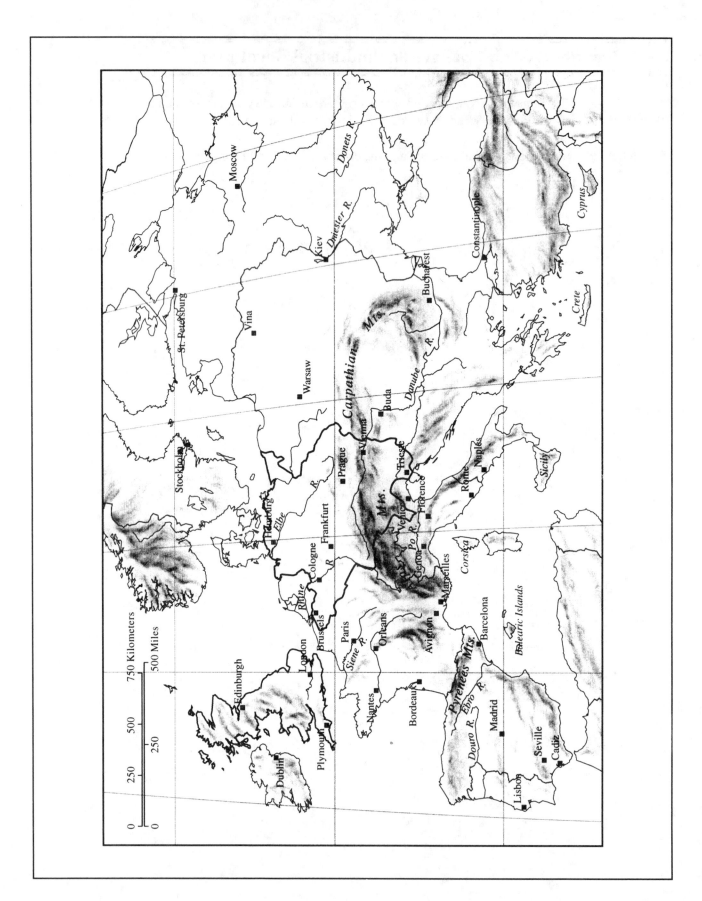

MAP 10

Locations

On Map 10 . . .

—Shade in the major manufacturing and industrial areas on the continent and Britain.

—In a different color, shade in or outline the areas on the continent and Britain that had developed railways by 1850.

Society and Environment

1.   Next to the following industries and sources of power, list the major associated regions.

Coal mining   _____

Iron industry   _____

Textile industry _____

Silk industry   _____

Banking   _____

2.   Name the three major centers on the continent where industrialization began.

_____
_____
_____
_____
_____

3.   What was the foundation of the industrial revolution in Britain?

_____
_____
_____
_____

4.   What were the environmental limitations on the development of the industrial revolution on the continent?

_____
_____
_____
_____
_____
_____

61

5.   What were some of the environmental consequences of the industrial revolution on the continent? England?

_____

_____

_____

_____

_____

_____

_____

6.   What were some of the social consequences of the industrial revolution on the continent? England?

_____

_____

_____

_____

_____

_____

_____

Early Modern Europe: Test Your Knowledge

Link the following city or region name on the left with the material goods, event, or development most appropriate to it on the right:

Amsterdam	16th century inflation rate of foodstuffs
Belgium	Cotton spinning mills
England	Exploration of west coast of Africa
Holy Roman Empire	Francs Bacon's Scientific Method
Kensington, London	Industrial fair
Mediterranean	Industrial investment banking
Midlands, Britain	Overthrow of the Aztecs
Portugal	Saint Bartholomew's Day massacre
Spain	Stock exchange
Vassy, France	Thirty Years' War

Extra Maps

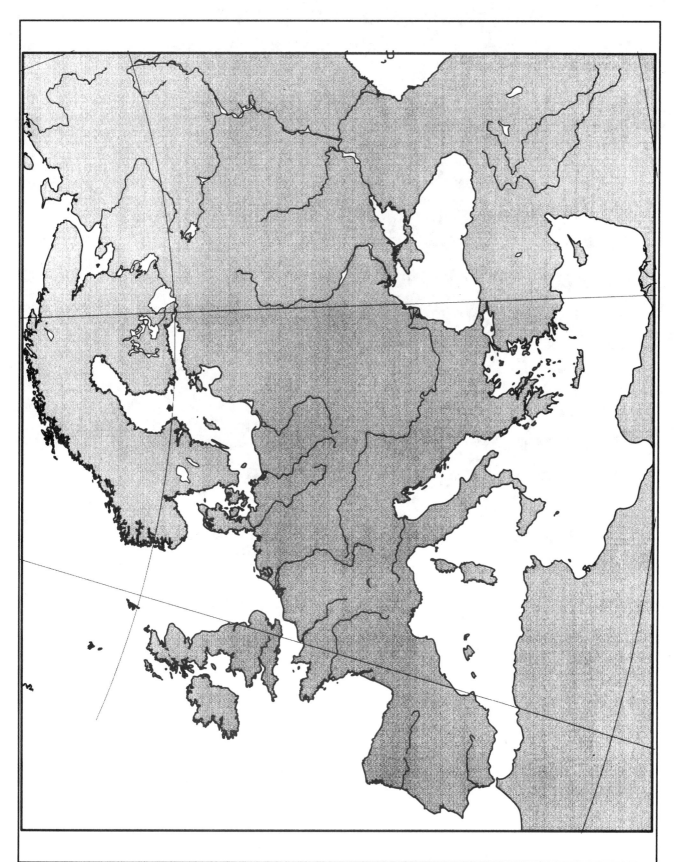

EUROPE

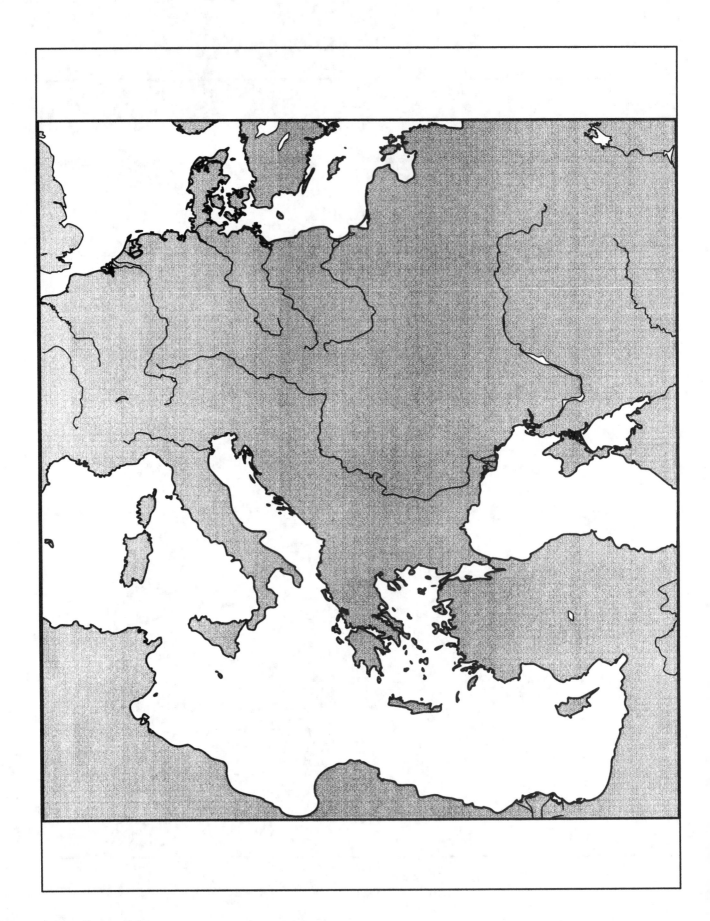

CENTRAL EUROPE

MEDITERRANEAN

Near East